Birds, Birds, Birds

Written and illustrated

by Martha Rohrer

Copyright 2004

Rod and Staff Publishers, Inc.
P.O. Box 3, Highway 172
Crockett, Kentucky 41413
Telephone (606) 522-4348

Printed in U.S.A.

ISBN 978-07399-2349-8
Catalog no. 2951

All the birds large and small
Make their own song or call.
 Their shapes do not all look the same.
When you see birds nearby
As they perch or they fly,
 How soon can you tell me their name?

What bird is always dressed
In brown, with orange breast?

You'll find the robin dressed
In brown, with orange breast.

Who will feed each baby bird
When their chirping cries are heard?

Soon the mother robin will
Bring a worm caught in her bill.

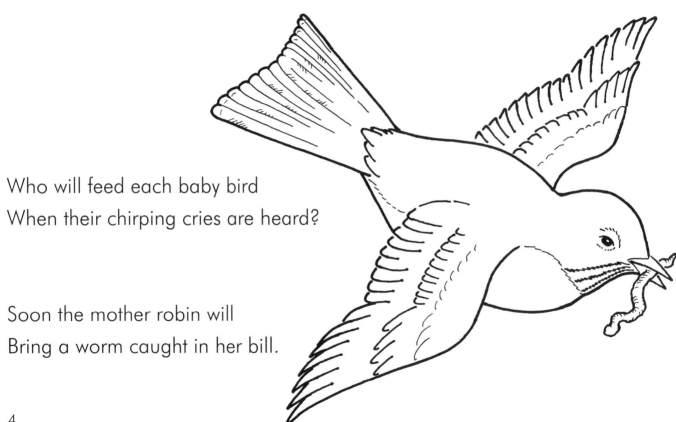

Who will eat the tasty worm
That can wiggle fast and squirm?

Hungry birdies in the nest
Will soon eat it all with zest.

What red bird sits and sings,
Then flies away on wings?

The cardinal sits and sings,
Then flies away on wings.

What green bird very small
Has the tiniest nest of all?

The hummingbird so small
Has the tiniest nest of all.

What is that red-capped bird
  When *tap, tap, tap* is heard?

A woodpecker is the bird
  When *tap, tap, tap* is heard.

What black-capped bird so free
Chirps "Chick-a-dee-dee-dee"?

The black-capped chickadee
Will chirp its name, you see.

In orange, black, and white,
What is this pretty sight?

The Baltimore oriole bright
Is such a pretty sight.

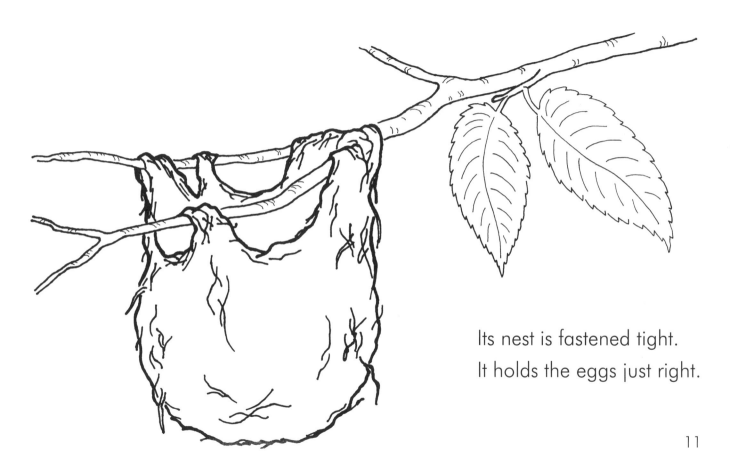

Its nest is fastened tight.
It holds the eggs just right.

What bird in coat of gray
Will look for seeds today?

Here comes the junco gray
To look for seeds today.

What bird in blue array
Drives other birds away?

Sometimes the noisy jay
Drives other birds away.

In black and yellow gown,
What bird finds thistledown?

The goldfinch likes to eat
The thistle's seedy treat.

What stands near that corn row?
It's black from head to toe.

There stands the cawing crow.
It flies in flocks, we know.

What bird with tail held high
May sing when we come nigh?

The busy, little wren
May sing so cheery then.

Its house,
   you can be sure,
Needs just
   a small round door.

What little bird creeps down?
Its head points to the ground.

A nuthatch will creep down.
Its head points to the ground.

What bird walks in the park?
It roosts when it gets dark.

The pigeon in the park
Will roost when it gets dark.

What bird sits in this tree?
It hunts at night, you see.

The owl sits in a tree.
It hunts at night, you see.

What bird sings clear and long,
"Whip-poor-will," its nighttime song?

The whip-poor-will sings long.
Its own name is its song.

What large bird in the sky
Will soar and glide so high?

The eagle in the sky
Will soar and glide so high.

From nests high in the tree,
What can the eaglets see?

Their view is far and wide
Across the countryside.

What bird along the shore
Will dive, or walk, or soar?

A gull along the shore
Will dive, or walk, or soar.

What tall birds stand and rest
In waters they like best?

Flamingos stand and rest
In waters they like best.

What bird is standing here
With family swimming near?

This mallard by the lake
Is a pretty-colored drake.

The ducklings swimming near
Stay with their mother here.

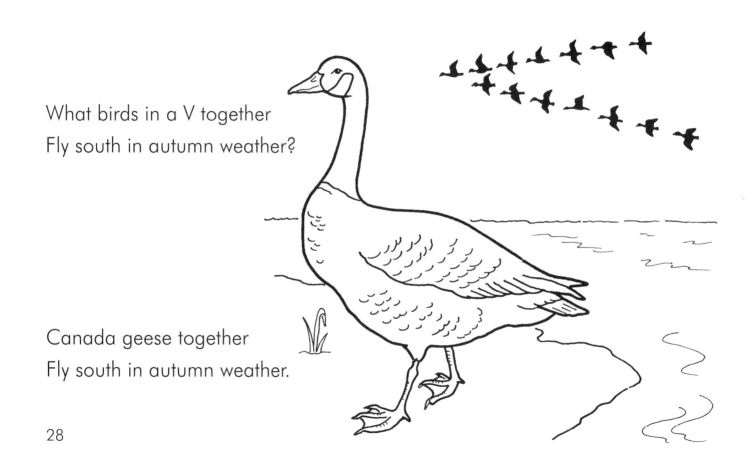

What birds in a V together
Fly south in autumn weather?

Canada geese together
Fly south in autumn weather.

With feathers spread so wide,
What bird is hard to hide?

A peacock spreads his fan
Of lovely feathers grand.

What brightly colored bird
Repeats another word?

The parrot in the jungle
May clearly speak, or mumble.

What bird sings cheerily?
It's in a cage, you see.

The sweet canary's song
Sounds cheery all day long.

Of all the birds so gay,
Can you draw one today?
Trace its head,
    and back,
    and breast.
Trace its tail.
Now add the rest.
Draw a beak,
    and wings,
    and feet.
Is your bird book
    now complete?